Does nothing rhyme with Charlbury?

Poems from a little town of stone

Does nothing rhyme with Charlbury?

Poems from a little town of stone

Compiled by Rob Stepney

*for Birgit
with love,
Michèle xxx*

THE WYCHWOOD PRESS

Our books may be ordered from bookshops or (post free) from
Evenlode Books, Market Street, Charlbury, OX7 3PH
01608 811969

e-mail: wychwood@joncarpenter.co.uk

Credit card orders should be phoned or faxed to 01689 870437 or 01608
811969

**A share of the proceeds from each copy sold will go to the
All Saints, Shorthampton appeal**

First published in 2006 by
The Wychwood Press
an imprint of Jon Carpenter Publishing
Alder House, Market Street, Charlbury, Oxfordshire OX7 3PH

ISBN-10   1 902279 27 1

ISBN-13   978-1-902279-27-5

Manufactured in England by LPPS Ltd., Wellingborough NN8 3PJ

Contents

Poets in alphabetical order

Adrian Lancini	Our local	81
Anthony Landale	Witness	25
John Lanyon	Alchemy of limestone	21
	Haiku and Improvisation in memoriam John Coltrane	63
	The shipwright says goodbye	45
	From my haiku box	100
	Something stronger	80
	On first looking into the oriental chill cabinet at Waitrose	108
Elma Marshall	The Charlbury cock and clock	24
M Mayhew	Loneliness	43
	Frustration	87
Dee Moss	The Beatitudes	52
Michele Nayman	It's in the detail	44
	Not always to our preferred design	46
	Proof	46
	Revelation	46
	Will not make you safe	116
Gillian Owen	Books and spaces	104
	I love my lampshade	104
	Cannes: Easter Day	76
Nick Owen	Falluja-in-Charlbury, a trilogy in search of a quartet	88
	A family of trees	19
	Millennium morn	28
	A walk among bluebells	60
Stuart Parker	Plumber's mate	118
Bill Parsons	Not just a memory but a living	83
Hilda Reed	Sestina: For a grandchild on a rainy day	38
	Hoard	39
	Sestina: Home is the sailor	55
Rob Stepney	Crayfishing	26
	What John Donne might have told…	62
	Not Adam's apple	75
	Vicar's ruin	80
	Fire and Ashes 2005	82
	Dangerous outside leaning	105
	It's all in the census	120

Introduction

If we think about what 'makes' contemporary poetry, disciplined rhyme and metre would certainly be a potential element, but only one among many possible characteristics. A feature of much poetic writing is that a few words carry great weight, often a heavy emotional charge which – though personally experienced – is wide in its implications. In trying fully to capture a sensation or feeling, certain poems put enough intensity into a moment to make it timeless. Poetry may be dense with layers of allusion and reference as authors seek to give insight into one thing by means of another.

But (especially to someone brought up on the Mersey poets of the 1960s) writing poems can also be about the joy and humour simply of playing with words. We let them go on holiday, test them out in unfamiliar roles.

This is a collection of poems about Charlbury by anyone, and by Charlbury people about anything. There's a great variety of form and content. Some is celebration. There's much on love, and more on loss. There's anger. And a bit on beer and cricket.

The unifying element is that – for one reason or another – people often feel like recording their feelings and experiences in a way that is… well, just not prose.

I am grateful to Hilda Reed and Ed Fenton for their help in compiling this book.

Rob Stepney
Charlbury, May 2006

I

River and stone

The Evenlode

HILAIRE BELLOC

I will not try to reach again,
I will not set my sail alone,
To moor a boat bereft of men
At Yarnton's tiny docks of stone.
But I will sit beside the fire,
And put my hand before my eyes,
And trace, to fill my heart's desire,
The last of all our Odysseys.
The quiet evening kept her tryst:
Beneath an open sky we rode,
And passed into a wandering mist
Along the perfect Evenlode.
The tender Evenlode that makes
Her meadows hush to hear the sound
Of waters mingling in the brakes,
And binds my heart to English ground.
A lovely river, all alone,
She lingers in the hills and holds
A hundred little towns of stone,
Forgotten in the western wolds.

Though born in France, Hilaire Belloc was educated at Balliol College,
Oxford, 1893-6. His biographer, A N Wilson, describes this poem as
immortalising Belloc's 'idyllic rambles by road and waterway' in the
surrounding countryside.

Charlbury, Bank Holiday Sunday, 2005

BRIGID ALLEN

Luminous with thistledown, the late August fields
lie tawny-dull or glittering in ochre stubble
as clouds pass over the wooded Sarsden ridge
in slate-thunder grey, in hard-edged, towering brightness.

Imagine how the town must seem from a balloon
as it drifts across on a still, spent Sunday evening,
when bonfire smoke makes a thin-blown, bitter cloud
and winnowing combine-dust could be stubble burning.

The ballooners look down on the stretched-out, lion's-pelt land,
the Evenlode, the church tower, the railway,
slate roofs, green trees, the blot of a copper beech,
roads heaving uphill out of the town, like symbols

on a three-dimensional map. Even the cars are unreal,
flashing down from the table-land to Chadlington.
Only buzzards circling, light-dipped, over Wychwood
inscribe on their paths of air that this is home.

Shorthampton

DAVID HALLIWELL

An extract from *Tom in Pam and Pam in Tom*

PAM	Oh love love love!
TOM	Oh love love love!
PAM	I can't live without you!
TOM	I can't live without you!
PAM	Listen I want to marry you
TOM	I want to marry you
PAM	I'll marry you in Shorthampton Church
TOM	I'll marry you in Shorthampton Church
PAM	Yes that wholesome
TOM	little church
PAM	near Charlbury
TOM	reached by a bridle path
PAM	nestling in the hills
TOM	and set amongst fields and flowers
PAM	and it'll be May
TOM	and there'll be blossom
PAM	and inside the church
TOM	in its simplicity
PAM	its peace and silence
TOM	we'll stand
PAM	side by side
TOM	hand in hand
PAM	before the plain
TOM	and pleasant altar
PAM	with the window behind it
TOM	looking out on green meadows
PAM	and woods and brown earth
TOM	a view which has been called
PAM	the most lovely altar cloth
TOM	in England.
PAM	And I'll say I do

TOM	And I'll say I do
PAM	and we will be married
TOM	and we will be married
PAM	deep
TOM	deep
PAM	in the
TOM	country
PAM	in that special
TOM	special place
PAM	with its old wall painting
TOM	on the south splay
PAM	of the squint
TOM	although we can
PAM	see it clearly
TOM	depicting the infant Jesus
PAM	making birds out of clay
TOM	and breathing life into them.
PAM	Yes and I
TOM	can imagine
PAM	the painting come alive
TOM	and leaving the wall
PAM	and the figures
TOM	the saviour
PAM	and the clay birds
TOM	beginning to move
PAM	and becoming vital
TOM	and vivid
PAM	and you are the saviour
TOM	and you are the saviour
PAM	and I'm a clay bird
TOM	and I'm a clay bird
PAM	and you put my beak
TOM	to your lips
PAM	and you gently blow
TOM	life into me
PAM	and as you blow
TOM	I grow.
PAM	Yes I am
TOM	the bird

PAM	we are
TOM	the bird
PAM	and
TOM	we grow
PAM	and we
TOM	flow
PAM	and
TOM	we fly
PAM	and we
TOM	soar
PAM	into
TOM	the future
PAM	and our
TOM	wings
PAM	are
TOM	our bonds
PAM	and we are free
TOM	we are free.

David Halliwell died in Charlbury in March 2006. The extract is reproduced by kind permission of Liz Antcliffe and Roger Halliwell. This, and the extract about Crawborough (p 66), also appear in the anthology In the Company of Poets, *ed John Rety, published by Hearing Eye in 2003.*

A family of trees

NICK OWEN

Mother, a massive enveloping oak
Dips her toes in the water
She looms out above the stream
With the sun like a bird on her shoulder
Her arms are stretched as wide as heaven
Her hair a vast wild mane

Father, a weird and ancient oak
A twisted wild wizard
Aloof
High above the bank
His head and shoulders are withered
Shrivelled
Almost dismembered
He is only alive through his high magic

The willow youth
Stands silently slender
Up to his single thigh in the swollen stream
Like a stork in motionless meditation

The toddlers
A cluster of mischievous thorns
Scrabble in the muddy hollow
All arms and legs and elbows
Having fun

Uncle has arms like tentacles
Snaking up and out and round
From his hideout
Below the bridge

He is a tree troll
His fingers
Drum on the parapet
A challenge to every traveller
Who walks his way

Charlbury Club Day

ROSA YOUNG

In the field of recreation
Opposite the aged turnpike
Stand a jumbled host of playthings
Stand the caravans and trailers
For the people congregate here
Every year about midsummer
Every year from town and hamlet
Coming in for Charlbury Club Day.
Friday evening, after sundown,
I can hear the music starting –
Starting up and getting louder
Till my eardrums split asunder.
Horses, Noah's Ark and Dodgems
Whirling round to strains of crooners,
Coconuts and shrieking women,
Gypsies selling squibs and windmills
Selling sweets to sticky children.
When at last the noise is over
Over for another twelvemonth,
People turn their faces homewards
Baskets packed with spoils they won there,
Sighing for another Club Day.

Alchemy of limestone

JOHN LANYON

The rain is acid
The stone is base
It fizzes and pops
Like a chemistry experiment
Like lemonade turning flat

This balancing-act of stones

He mixes the mortar
He fills the gaps
Soft as butter
Yellow as butter
Everyday
'You can't build a house of butter'
He warns me

The sheep left
The shepherd danced away

The rain fills the cracks
Freezes
Splits the stone
It moves and falls

The earth resists the spade

House-prices rise

This is home
This little house
This pile of stones
This is our dream
Melting away

The optimistic man says
'Just wait for the sun to come out
Just wait'

Dedication to Vernon Watney

JOHN BUCHAN

We two confess twin loyalties –
Wychwood beneath the April skies
Is yours, and many a scented road
That winds in June by Evenlode.
Not less when Autumn fires the brake,
Yours the deep heath by Fannich's lake,
The corries where the dun deer roar
And eagles wheel above Sgurr Mór.
So I, who love with equal mind
The southern sun, the northern wind,
The lilied lowland water-mead
And the grey hills that cradle Tweed,
Bring you this tale which haply tries
To intertwine our loyalties.

Reproduced by kind permission of A P Watt Ltd on behalf of The Lord Tweedsmuir and Jean, Lady Tweedsmuir.

In 1921, John Buchan (then living at Elsfield) began his novel Midwinter, *part of which is set in Cornbury Park. Vernon Watney, owner of the park, had given Buchan a copy of his book* Cornbury and the Forest of Wychwood *(1910) and Buchan was a frequent visitor. He dedicated his novel, set around the 1745 Jacobite rebellion, to Watney.*

Walcot walls

SARAH GEESON-BROWN

I am building a wall,
a task that cannot be hurried.

Each dry stone is placed
by hand, no
weak spots or careless
joins. Like blind justice,
I balance their weight and judge their size.
Then carefully sentence each rock
to life with its neighbour.

The stones themselves have previous lives,
creatures calcified, flora fossilised.
And now imprisoned within the wall
A choir of lithic voices sing earth's eternal round.

I am building a wall,
a task that cannot be hurried.

Between my neighbour's land and mine,
It stands thus, $\div$, a universal sign
To show the wall divides us either side.
Careless work makes cracks and seams
Where rocks can stress and strain.
But as I work I hear the choir's harmony,
And as I knit the stones from side to side
they form a thread
which weaves our lives,
and thus creates a solid tapestry.

The Charlbury cock and clock

Elma Marshall

*For me, Charlbury has always been a special place – an oasis in the dark.
After a teaching career, I attempted an Open University degree. One day,
making heavy weather of an essay, I sat gazing at St Mary's Church and
composed a poem. I seemed to get renewed inspiration. The view from my
window did the trick.*

The cockerel stands on Mary's Tower
A very fine bird is he
With his golden plumes and bright red comb
He's a very rare sight to see.

I watch him from my window
As he looks to east and west
Sometimes it seems he can't decide
What's really for the best.

He sees the people as they pass
To worship, work or play
He's proud and regal, lord of all
'A King', you might well say.

Without a sound, he takes command
And points us to the way
The wind is blowing hard or soft
For a calm or stormy day.

Below him hangs his golden friend
A round and noisy clock
That tells us all the time of day
A rival for the cock.

He does his duty very well
With his Roman Numbers face

But now and then his chimes don't work
And then he's in disgrace.

I like to hear him striking
I know that all is well
He makes me joyful, makes me think
A happy tale to tell.

The years will pass and things will change
But after I am gone
I hope the Cockerel and the Clock
Will yet live on and on.

Witness

ANTHONY LANDALE

Be still and let the river come to you.
All your reaching will not get you there.
Be still. But stay awake and the swallows
And martins will fly to you. Connected by the
Invisible attention that is the thread you
Have been looking for and following.

For once you do not have to explain.
You do not have to compare. It is enough
To witness, to see that the patterns in the
Clouds and the currents in the water are
Brushed by the same hand. And that hand
Has everything and nothing to do with you.

Crayfishing

ROB STEPNEY

In September 2000, Alan Fraser took me crayfishing for the first time. It happened to coincide with the death of the last of the infamous Kray twins, gangsters who had terrorised East London.

An adventure at dusk by Pudlicote bridge
In a rising Evenlode mist
Humans and river crustaceans
In a traditional Autumn tryst

Meshes of metal slung from a string
A pig heart wired to the grill
Bait for Ronnie and Reggie
Who would both be keen for the kill

Soft splash in swift-flowing stream
Then the trap sinks down to the mud
There's a wait that seems too long to bear
While the creatures sense the blood

As the grill's hauled up over forked stick
Dark scorpion shapes cling to the flesh
A fumbling attempt keeps them there
Until the bucket is under the mesh

Shaken off and imprisoned they scrabble around
Waving East-end boxers' claws
Tangled feelers as long as themselves
And scavenging, gangster jaws

If there's nothing else, they'll eat each other
To any sense of morality numb
Primitive but highly successful
And by reputation kind to their mum

Back home in the boiling, salted pot
Their sludge colour changes to red
There's a convulsive movement or two
Though they're clearly already dead

Sweet nuggets of flesh in the armoured tail
Are good, though nothing like lobster
But there's a scrap to be found in the pincers too
And that's enough for a mobster.

The native crayfish, which is protected, is small and black. You are much more likely to find the introduced American species, which is large and has red claws.

Millennium morn

NICK OWEN

Woke to sunshine
Streaming out of a new millennium

Buzzing with energy
Bubbling with joy

I had to be out there
In the world of nature
Glorious sunshine
Glorious new world
Glorious new day

Pedalling out
Face to face with the sun himself
Flooding Market Square
Beaming in the delight of his own being
Squatting at the end of Sheep Street
Over Hixet Wood

Delicate gossamer strands of mist
Floated just feet above the fields.

The Evenlode
Brimming with rain
Brimming with trout
Rushing out of Charlbury
Butting under Rotherwick's bridge

Tender soft cold caress of
Not quite icy mist
Hanging from sunbeams
In the cradle of the valley

Oh to be a millennium babe,
Born out of water
Into the sparkling, shining,
Rising-sun day

The single magpie heralded closed gates
Black iron gargoyled faces
Tearing up our invitations
To walk in Cornbury Park on New Year's Day

But all the land was sun-kissed
Under a soft sky,
As the road eased out to Stonesfield
And the remnants
Of Wychwood's primeval forest.

This millennium
So very well met,
The most beautiful morning
Of this winter, yet.

No, I don't remember Adlestrop

BOB COCKBURN

Yes, I remember Charlbury
and a station from my youth.
Once, as a youth, I stayed there,
but only remember a view.

Yes, I remember Charlbury
where the train was not on time.
Yes, I remember Charlbury,
for which I could not find a rhyme.

Older, a parent, I came again,
thinking, 'How we change' –
had coffee with a one-time love,
felt distant. Cold. Strange.

Yes, I remember Charlbury,
where the train was not on time.
Yes, I remember Charlbury,
but I still can't find a rhyme.

But, now the timing's right,
I keep coming back again,
for music, friends and stimulus –
I still sometimes come by train.

The best of the old
the best of the new
a place between times –
with, now, a wider view.

Yes, I remember Charlbury
where the train was not on time.
Yes, I remember Charlbury –
don't think I'll ever find that rhyme.

Charlbury names, in rhyme

Fiction is strange, but facts more strangely fall,
And CHARLBURY NAMES eclipse in strangeness all.
Pass we then, reader, thro' each lane and street,
And mark the curiosities we meet.
Ascending from the Railway, first we note
A TAYLOR lives who never made a coat.
In Market Street what wonders on us pour,
Behold a DRAPER there who deals in Flour.
And at the entry of the street we stop,
Amazed to find a BASKETT keeping shop.
While, to increase the wonder of our stare,
A FARMER shaves you, or curtails your hair.
On t'other hand there doth exist the Charmer,
A COOPER, who by business is a farmer.
With sweetest smile pervading all his face,
A MILLER offers ribbons, tapes and lace.
(That placid smile the consequence, 'tis said,
Of leaving every fear, at least ALDRED).
And of these prodigies the list to close,
A COLLIER stands the landlord of the Rose. (& Crown).
In Church Street, too, believe me, 'tis no myth,
A banker, druggist, grocer is a SMITH …

This is the first part of a long poem attributed to Dr Clifton when first published in Jesse Clifford's My Reminiscences of Charlbury *(c1892). It is reproduced in John Kibble's* Charlbury and its Nine Hamlets *(1927).*

Invitations to the Fair

Charlbury Museum has Street Fair programmes dating back to 1957. The first two poems below are from 1973.

THE BARD OF HIXET (FRANK DUNN)

Lords and ladies, lads and lasses!
If the weather should be fine,
Throng the Charlbury streets in masses
On September twentynine.

Come from every nook and cranny
To this most fantastic Fair.
Parents, kids and even Granny
All will find amusement there.

When you pause before each sideshow,
On your spending set no curb.
All – it cannot be denied – show
Ingenuity superb.

In the evening, gay and gaudy
Are the fancy dress and floats –
Some perhaps a little bawdy,
Raising cheers from vulgar throats.

And at last, when all is silent
And each pub has closed its door
Think: the fun, so fast and violent,
Comes again in 'sevntyfour.

GWYN TUDOR

The theme for this year's Street Fair is the one of Carnival,
And we hope you'll all dress up and join the fun.
There are stalls and exhibitions, races, competitions, draws,
Fancy Dress parades, with room for everyone.

Caribbean Steel Band playing, Morris Dancers on the hop,
Hot dogs and toffee apples by the score;
Polish Folk Dance, Johnnie Chuckles, and a Carnival Masked Ball.
We feel sure that you could ask for little more.

The 1897 Charlbury vaccination riot

(As described by Lois Hey in A History of Charlbury*)*

IAN COX

They passed a Law in '53, to give us jabs, to keep us well.
But some kids died, or so we heard.
My Dad said : 'No, he's well enough.'
And so did nine more in our Town.

The Police came round in '97, to take our things, to pay the fine.
The auction set for half past twelve.
My Dad said 'No.' They took him in.
They took our stuff, to sell for bids.

The Town Cryer cried at half past twelve, could not be heard, the
crowd too loud.
The brass band played, to drown the bids.
The Town said 'No', except one man.
The bidder fell, they dragged him down.

The Trumpet played at half past one, in a policeman's ear, to start a fight
With rotten eggs, mud, flour and rice.
The auction moved to Playing Close,
To no avail, to make the peace.

A bag of flour, by two o'clock, had fallen on the gaveller's head.
The ghostly figure, looking dead.
Had had enough, and sped for home.
The Police went too: 'See you in court!'

They went to court July that year, to go to jail, or so we thought.
'We only went to hear the band.'
A great defence, they got off free.
The Law repealed, a Victory.

Your Grandad could be one of those men.
'It couldn't happen today,' he'd say.
Ask those who know about these things
Of jabs and cures and Laws and stuff.

Ballad of Charlbury Street Fair
1976

{The yeare of the Greate Drought, and constant Sonne Finally broken by Greate Raine. Aug 30 1976. J.G.

Key G Allegro.

Tom Fowler Tom Fowler lend me you grey mare To cart round the tradesmen of Charl-bur-ee Fur they wants for

Tom Fowler Tom Fowler lend me your Grey Mare
To cart round the tradesfolk of Charl-bur-ee
Fur they wants fur to go to Charlbury St Fair.
With: Jack Cowley. Bill Goodgame Rossie Alder
H. Perkins. Butcher Chapman, Vera Atkins Miss Burnage
Yvonne {Old Vic Brackenbury <u>and all</u>}. Repeat

Well now! - you've put me in a bit of a 'ole
  (She's the gayest old Nag in all Charl-bur-ee)
And I've got an idea she's expecting a foal
So try Dave Coles, George Parsons John Phillips
Peter Sullivan, Dicky Worth .
(They'll provide you with transport and all) (Repeat

But Tom these good chaps they all wants some 'ard cash
(We ain't too well feathered in Charl-bur-ee)
Come on wi' ye misers and 'ave a real splash
There's Midland and Barclays. Cashier Harris
Pretty Jenny, young Avis. Petronella and
      Manager Tom Crane and all. (repeat.)

So they went to the Banks and they drew on the till
  (Twas almost like Wall St in Charl-bur-ee.)
Then round every pub they went a'taking their fill
At The Marlborough. The Railway. The White Hart The Bell
The Bull (That new bloke on Bull corner) and all. (repeat.)

So all you good people as comes to our Fair
A welcome from us 'ere in Charl-bur-ee
May you 'ave a good time wi' us while you be yur
Till you goes back to Stonesfield and Fawler and
Spelsbury and Ramsden Finstock (even Oxford)
  A rattlin' good time to ye all. (repeat)

Printed at the house near St Marys church
of one Adrian Lack Printer 1976.   BROADSHEET by   Wandering Versifier
                                                   Bridget Wastie

From the 1976 Street Fair programme.

35

II

Love and loss

Sestina: For a grandchild on a rainy day

The garden shivers, wet with driving rain.
You come into the kitchen warm and bright
to paint your vibrant thoughts with rainbow hands
on sugar paper, pink or blue or red,
your choices sure, your concentrating breath
rocking a feather grafted on a star.

Mallard, Flying Scotsman, Evening Star?
A carriage window steaming in the rain
or misting over with your eager breath;
a tender coupled to the gleaming, bright
and streamlined engine, liveried in red,
the journey starts, the train in steady hands.

The train in orbit now, your hectic hands
break down a tower built to reach a star,
they scatter bricks and blocks in brilliant red
and varnished arcs, descending like a rain
of wooden ice cubes, clattering on the bright
and polished floor. You freeze and hold your breath.

'Come now! I think you'd better stop for breath
and have some tea.' I watch your nimble hands
absorbed in sorting cheese from bacon, bright
red apple chunks from crumbling pastry stars.
Outside the cat-flap clatters in the rain,
a car draws up, its brake lights glistening red.

Home at last, your parents back, red
from running through the rain. With laughing breath
you have your bath: the splashes like the rain-
drops on the window, steam wreathing your hands;
your shampooed hair in tufts. A spiky star
you shine out from the towel, dry and bright.

Finishing a drink, and with the bright
lights dimmed, you choose a story that's been read
to you a hundred times before, its star
a giant, or a train. Your indrawn breath
is held as pictures travel through your hands
and words begin to merge with driving rain.

The story told, your bright eyes closed, your breath
warm as the soft, red blanket in your hands;
a shooting star falls silent in the rain.

A sestina consists of six verses, each of six lines, plus a concluding verse of three lines. The final words of each line in the first verse also appear as line-endings in the next five verses, but each time in a different sequence. The short concluding verse contains all six final words.

Hoard

HILDA REED

I covet the softness of your fingers,
tell them with my own scarred, bone-hard hands,
hoard them with mine in my pocket;
count them mine in the long term.

And then you pass me by

Igor Goldkind

For Natasha Zuniga Hudson, my darling little sister.
January 29, 2005

I've known you for two, then three, followed by four and five, now
    six lifetimes.
First you and me, then our children and you know, it's always been
    the same:

You stop, you turn, you smile
And then you pass me by.

On a stretch of unpaved road in the middle of nowhere,
Standing on wet cobblestones reflecting amber lights,
In the City of Light living amongst the pigeons,
On the steps of the pyramid pointed at the sun,
In our mother's arms.
In my garden, near the overgrown bamboo, next to the fountain I
    would never build,
On a treadmill at the Berkeley Y,
At the children's zoo, riding atop the great tortoise shell,
On the carousel of every airport in the world looking for our lost
    luggage,
In the stations of the North, the East and the West,
On a train without tickets, heading to Rome without money:

You stop, you turn, you smile
And then you pass me by.

In New York eating Jewish food round the corner from a shop where
    our grandfather cobbled shoes.
On the Monkey bars, in the playground just behind our two story
    apartment.
In the back seat of a pale blue Ford Cortina coming back from a
    scary Dizzy-Land,
Your yellow balloon bobbing precariously near the open window

My heart perched to fly out with it into the madness and the freedom,
You were watching, just watching me.
Every night in front of the evening news watching bodies count,
In the afternoon sun on the warm floor of your Oakland bungalow,
Waiting for a visa.
Laughing at the funny parts in Leonard Cohen songs.
Talking politics, talking about small change.
In a pub, outside Cork, drinking Guinness, a creamy moustache
    under your nose.
In the gallery on the left bank where you worked
Selling masks to rich Americans.
While I drank too much red wine at the zinc counter in the café
    across the road:

You stop, you turn, you smile
And then you pass me by.

On the West coast, past the last coast on a Greyhound taking us home
At the train station on a platform, past the ticket office with no more
    money to get to Rome
At the post office, near the bakery, in the phone box calling mom.
At King Arthur's castle, near Merlin's cave, your sons dancing on the
    waves,
Breaking into your piggy bank for marijuana money and finding the
    ha-ha, caught-ya note you wrote instead.
In the train carriage when I saved you from the German punk wearing
    the dog collar whose bare room we spray-paint day-glow together.
Every argument I ever had with our mother.
Pulling our father's hands off our mother's neck while you cowered in
    the corner.
Hearing you learn to speak Spanish then French so much better than
    me.
Dancing on Stimson beach with our mother and my wife, one hand
    in the air,
Scrutinized by our children,
Your heart that day, an ocean big enough to swallow all of us and the
    Sun.
Meeting your future husband the last day you would ever be my little
    sister again:

You stop, you turn, you smile
And then you pass me by.

Meeting my wife for the first time and telling me how good she was
    and would be.
Flying all the way to London for my wedding, my best friend in the
    whole wild world.
Then me nearly getting you arrested in a mad car driven by an
    Indian physicist.
Convincing me that being a father didn't mean having to be our
    father.
Making plans in the sand for our mother so she could veto them over
    and over again
(Constant as the waves).
On the phone every once and awhile comparing attitudes towards a
    film, an art exhibit or simply swapping curses about the government.
Standing by me, believing in me even when I'd nearly given up.
Seeing your first son for the first time standing, staring silently at me.
In the hospital beyond all hope where I woke up to your blue
    puzzled eyes, to realise, indelibly, like a freight train what my life
    was really worth:

And then, the phone ringing,
 in the morning while I boot my disc for the millionth time.
Your husband's voice on the telephone.
Igor, Listen to me
Oh god, your new baby's died!
Igor, Listen to me.
(No).
You stop,
(No).
Igor, Listen to me
You turn.
No.
Listen to me.

You smile.

And then you pass me by.

Loneliness

M MAYHEW

In the park on the corner
A long time ago
You kissed me one autumn.
How could I know

Our nights would be many
Our days would be long?
What have I now
Of that first lonely song?

I have nothing to show
No material gain
The days are still long
But the song is the same.

The rose in the garden
My thoughts in the dark
Are a way to remember
The kiss in the park.

You are part of me now
That no-one can share
Two halves of a whole.
Did we build something rare?

Time blows the flame out.
Alone – I cannot show
That I love you more now
Than I did long ago.

It's in the detail

MICHELE NAYMAN

It's in the detail life is lived,
the picking up from school;
the way a lunch is packed with fruit,
a jacket when it's cool.

It's in a smile affection lies,
not gestures grand or wild;
love is learned from the time and care
a parent gives a child.

A parent hard or cold creates
a child who cannot cry;
sadness will take hold and grow
and blanket out the sky.

All of what we do or don't
is how we leave our trace;
no accolades or cash reward
can match a child's embrace.

The shipwright says goodbye

JOHN LANYON

Where the flames meet the waves
Let her go, let her go
Tide take her, trembling
Tide take her

Where the river runs deep
As night falls
Let her go, let her go

Chains, shackles and pulleys

Commend her to the Fates
Let her go, let her go

She sails to the West
The past claims its coin –
Her amber, her silver, her gold

Tide take her

She's got a new man now

Not always to our preferred design

MICHELE NAYMAN

Those of us whose spirit levels are faulty,
who therefore cannot always draw
a straight line through life,
are handicapped carpenters
but capable, perhaps, of building cabinets with
unusual angles, secret compartments,
strange reflective surfaces.

If you like your furniture built of oak,
or strictly at ninety degrees,
I may not be for you.
But if you know that the rooms we live in
are not always to our preferred design:
welcome. Here's my guest book. Sign.

Proof

The mathematics of belief
involves imaginary numbers;

but the equation must balance
if it is to be usable at all.

Revelation

Do not confuse calm
with indifference.

The world manifests itself best
to those who are still.

Country funeral: epitaph for a young plumber

FREDDIE JONES

The unremarkable, indifferent trees
Busily juggle the fragile light
Through antique windows
Virginalised of illumined saint,
Of coloured prophesy,
Of promised history,
By time, or chance,
Or bland indifference;
But here sit the mourning Quick
Brittle,
Coldly awaiting
The tardy corpse;
Their mortality nakedly impatient
For emancipation
From their great,
Their imponderable loss.

Inordinate
How waiting anger turns
From death to
Organist, young
And earnestly betraying
The dirge,
Now satirical of Death,
A Mockery of Life.

And now, at last, the corpse,
Garlanded in cliche,
But drenched in prayered redemption
Smugly packaged and
Richly privy
To the dark bewildering
Of Death.

Leaving,
An orgy of improbable
Shytouchingacceptedembracing,
Alien in the light of Life,
But now, in silent rejoice,
Congratulatory,
In one more escape
From the Beckoning.

Swing me

D Moira Wyatt

Swing me Gran, swing me
Higher and higher – up to the sky.
Swing me, please swing me,
I need wings to fly
Where the clouds are all golden
And the sun's shining bright,
Till I melt away – away –
In the sparkling sunlight.

Don't stop Gran – keep swinging,
I must quickly float on
Where the wild birds are winging,
Until the day's done.
Over trees and the high hills
I'm flying – I'm flying.
Suddenly Gran's gone,
The swings dying and dying.

The ballpoint

D Moira Wyatt

How can this pen with balled end tell
Of Nature in her wildest moods,
Or paint the craggy rock or fell,
And Autumn's colours in the woods?

Where is the breadth of sensuous line
To draw to mind the soft and sweet
Of evenings spent with thee and wine,
And curtains drawn against the street?

The sharp point cannot draw a veil
Of misty mornings by the sea
Impossible to write about
The things that you have said to me.

The words lie flat, the ink grows thin,
And time will fade all this.
The ghostly wording onward goes
Until the ink no longer flows.

Not even God can save her

PETER HEAD

for Jane Atkinson

Down to the beach
Near a harbour I forgot
See the sun on the horizon
It's blistering hot

This is the beach
When I was a kid
I came a lot
It'll be cold in the cave
Is it OK if we stop?

Down on the beach
Paw prints in the sand
Enjoying the coast
Where the sea meets the land

Watch the waves grow
God's only daughter
Got dragged out to sea
In the rough water

Down in the rock pools
God's angel swims
Catch the reflection
Of her brightly coloured fins

Down in the rock pools
God's angel sings
This is where her life ended
And this is where it begins

Splashing and crashing
Hear the waves shout
And follow her whispers
As the tide moves out

No-one can save her
As she slowly drifts out
There's no-one around
To hear her shout

It warms my heart
To hear her sing
Accompanied by the whistles
Of the caves and the wind

Lots of people
Swallowed by the sea
Lots of lonely hearts
Expect you home for tea

Kept by the sea
In your own little bay
Mum's waiting for a call
To let her know you're OK

The Beatitudes

DEE MOSS

They clustered round Him on the grassy mound,
The poor in spirit, and the hungry poor,
The meek and those who mourn.
(Was He in grief for Jo, his earthly Dad?)

He knew that some were longing to be right with God,
He recognised the pure in heart,
The men of peace,
And some whose lives were never quite at rest
Because of torment for their steadfast faith.

He told them all, 'Cheer up,
Rejoice, Be glad!
For God has great rewards for you.
You shall be called His children,
Yes, His very sons and daughters.
He will comfort you
And you will one day claim
The Kingdom of my Father, God.'

And still Christ knows us, every one,
Our doubts and woes,
Our longing to be right with God.
His promises hold firm,
For us the joyful certainty is here.
We all will find His comfort and His love.
We too, can claim the Kingdom of our God.

The Beatitudes

JOHN BOWERS

Behold the moon!
If new or full, we know, although we cannot see it
That there is light or dark, in balance, on the farther side.
And so is much of life:

A shaft of sunlight shows us heaven and lifts depression of the spirit;
In mourning, comfort comes, perhaps from unexpected source;
In asking not too much, we find we gain all that we want or need.
Hunger for peace and justice shared
Brings help from fellow pilgrims on that quest.
Mercy is granted to us, not from merit but because we once were
    merciful.

When worldly thoughts are held at bay, we find we can see God,
In making peace, we know that we have kinship with our God,
No evil force can quench our spirit, keep us from our God.

These are not pious hopes of future bliss;
The eye of faith can see their substance now.
God may work in mysterious ways;
His purpose is made real through actions of our love.

*The above two poems were written by members of the 2005 'Churches
Together in Charlbury' Lent afternoon group.*

Saturday

Jessica von Kaenel

With the people drawn away the landscape
Is old-fashioned.
I walk through the grey, gummy soup of Saturday.

In the stillness of the washing room I pause.
Every aloneness is really two alonenesses:
By the gummy wadding of Saturday I am insulated from others.

In the stillness of the washing room I pause:
Something not of Saturday comes swelling back.
The intransigent insulation of days separates me from all
That is not Saturday: the last exam,
Home, my cat, my parents and
The books I want to read; a less oppressive quiet,
an indefinable lightness in the sky – but the days are countable.

I can wear them down just by living.

Tomorrow will be Sunday; Sundays
have a quiet, still life of their own,
But Saturday is the cold leftovers of the week, a halfhearted stew
    served tiredly
by a giantess who barely cares.

Saturday creates a centre of perfect aloneness.

Sestina: Home is the sailor

HILDA REED

On Sundays, when the Queen might come to tea,
they spread the white and gleaming damask cloth
and stroked the monogram, like silken string,
that told its provenance in satined red:
Red Ensign Club, the homeless sailors' home,
provided by the doorman, from the store.

And other gifts came to them from the store:
porridge and biscuits, Mazzawattee tea,
taken by the doorman to their home,
the contraband disguised in dusty cloth,
a coarsely woven flag, its ground of red
bearing a Union Jack, and tied with string.

At breakfast time, the porridge, laced with strings
of glowing syrup melted from the store,
fills the child with warmth; the doorman red
from worrying the stove to make the tea
that splashes from the saucer to the cloth,
worn and well washed and smelling now of home.

The father, doorman, at the Sailors' Home,
collects another parcel tied with string.
The mother, meanwhile, spreads the tea-stained cloth
for dinner: bread and dripping from the store
of goods, dwindling now to porridge and some tea;
the flag hangs in the corner, limp and red.

At tea time with the fire glowing red
within the blackened stove, the father home
with currant biscuits in a jar for tea,
binding the handle of his knife with string
taken from the parcel from the store,
they laugh and smooth the tired damask cloth.

The smooth-embroidered, Sunday, damask cloth,
the letters R E C in fading red;
the rambling C a G she thinks, her store
of knowledge growing in the sailor's home:
George Rex, Elizabeth, entwined like string,
because today the Queen might come to tea.

The damask cloth lies in the sailor's home,
the red bled out and fraying now like string.
The store is empty. There will be no tea.

Eyes down looking for a full house

JESSICA VON KAENEL

In a temperature which is to heat and cold
What quiet is to silence and noise; a bit closer to one than the other
In a lull beneath
the dull thunderous rotation of the days
The clock's tick a heartbeat in the cloudy suspension;
My cat is energy in the still hall;
Unaware of how alone a force
she is in the oppressiveness of the still house,
Its air within the lightly heavy suspension
Of air and breathing
And silence and clock ticking, as yet unspeaking and level
Loneliness of a place
Left discreetly alone by futures and the grand glamour of improbable
    events,
Breathing the warm dust in the beams,
they dance
Mindlessly because they have no minds which is very
Alone-making

The motes swirl, the clock ticks, she pounces
Doggedly, exaggeratedly, frenziedly on a limp toy
(like a child whose intensity of need
commands the body to squeeze from within
convulsions of exhausting manufactured ecstasy and leaving him
harrowed through
with dismay and a tiredness like grief –
somehow, surely, she must feel it too?)

There was a time when this toy was bright new fabric.
That was something vaguely alive,
determined, colour and stiffness and tight precise stitching
– integrity!

That toy was something definite then.

57

Now things have sagged, gone ropey and limp.
No vivid, plural, tiny life abounds, it is shabby
And used, endlessly exhaustedly breathing the breath of 'no surprises'

The motes dance, the clock ticks,
– she pounces –
the warm floor
Is cautiously momentous to bare feet.

Loneliness

D MOIRA WYATT

'I am no use,' he says,
The old man, pale of face.
'What can I do
But hang about the place
Where I was born?
The others have it now.
New life echoes in it.
I only slow their pace
And show dispirit.
My mind is not the same.
My books are misty too –
It's time to go,' he said,
From lips both cracked and blue.

Spin

DAVID WHITTAKER

(i.m. Stafford Beer)

> *And here, quiet now lies the quarry*
> *below the twilight arch*

Abandoned shadows spinning,
    silently echo cryptic intimations
reverberating wall to wall
    in this hushed hidden cell

August wind freshly stirs
    the sweet incense, charred and
dying daily, daily dying,
    embers of an ashen altar sighing

> *still spinning…spinning still*

The hourglass suspends its
    turning game, weaving space into
time-tied threads, meeting a deadline
    just this side of forever and never, again

> *still spinning…spinning still*

Untamed, the garden of the brain
    tended by a tender heart of plenitude,
where dappled shades interplay
    and butterflies gorgeously display

> *(a circumspect owl gives a startled hoot*
> *from the void: to-wit-to-woo to you too old pal)*

The still-point of the spinning wheel
    embalms and calms sweet emblems
of desire to be without desire,
    as journey's endgame begins to recur

And here, the transit of absence marks
a tutelary presence, below the twilight arch

spinning still…spinning still…still spinning…

Spin *is an elegy for my friend Stafford Beer, a professor of cybernetics. Strongly influenced by Gandhi to the extent that spinning wool became a form of meditation for him, he taught Tantric yoga and was immersed in Vedantic metaphysics. He was also a poet and a painter. Part of each year he lived quietly in a remote cottage in an old quarry in the Welsh hills near Lampeter.*

A walk among bluebells

Nick Owen

Ours were silk-soft shoe steps
Sinking
In a shimmering sea of bluebells
Luxuriating
In spring's serene sunshine

For moments we were like sunbeams
Dancing among the shadowy boughs

For a while
We bathed in each other's love

We were like fishes
Flashing freely through the rippling flowers

In eternity
We could have been
Adam and Eve

In that first paradise

Before knowingness
Tore us out of Nature
Into time and dying.

Let love live

Peter Head

Did you see me
Disappear?
When I went
Did you shed a tear?

Thanks for coming
My day of rest
Here's to life
All the best

Thanks for coming
It's time to rest
This has been my life
I've given it my best

Look after my loved ones
I leave behind
And let them know
They're on my mind

Look after my loved ones
I leave behind
Look after my loved ones
They've been so kind

Thanks for coming
My day of rest
We have issues to look at
Problems to address

Thanks for coming
It's time to rest
We have issues to look at
My life's a mess

Thanks for coming
Time to forgive
Time for each other
To love and let live

What John Donne might have told the Corinthians

Rob Stepney

O Death, where is thy prick?
In that lies thy sting.

When all is said and done

Jessica von Kaenel

God is the invisibility in the corner,
The white eclipse in the mind's eye.
Sometimes the thing crafted by
the deep song of the organ and stained air,
the sober chords of sweetness and still light,
the stately dance to the altar
God is what remains
When all is said and done.

Haiku and improvisation in memoriam John Coltrane

JOHN LANYON

Jumping from the head
Blue notes fall like silver leaves
The wild horse comes home

Blue head-notes
Jumping
Silver horses, leaving home
This is the head-wind
The hurricane
Silver head, blue head
Wild head
Jumping, pushing, falling
Horse head
It's autumn in New York
Head wild, horse wild
Silver wild
Leaves like notes
Scrawled
At night-fall
At note- fall
Jump-blues, home-blues
Love blues
Blues falling
With a feeling
Like rain, the silver rain
The wild rain
Coming home, coming home
Crying home
Riding the wild horse
Riding the leaves
Flying home

The wild horse comes home
Blue notes fall like silver leaves.

Daedalus afraid to fly

Igor Goldkind

David, you bastard, you've left me
Understanding here alone,
With only these words falling out of my hands,
When it is yours I want to hear again.
Words of your mastery, not mine.

So what was all the swearing about then, David?
What were all those Northern fumes really burning from?
I told you the songs of Yorkshire would never play in LA
(Or London, for that matter):
Two towns equidistant from your Yorkshire mother.

Why didn't you just sell out?
You could have bought yourself a much better pint of beer
With all that money for old knotted ropes and
Still have coughed your asthmatic laughter at us all.

Is Death your idea of some kind of joke?
Did you finally track down the film rights to Malcolm, David,
And cash them in?
Are you really, secretly living in Barbados,
Making beautiful women miserable?
The obits are all for tax purposes and Death missed its mark again?
To think of all this wasted sorrow and
Empty glasses of beer.

You did say you always wanted to visit other places.
But Daedalus was afraid to fly.
If you had been born upside down in America
You would have been a southern writer living in some Northern
    town.
Spilling your southern drawl over a rum and coke in a New York
    City Bar.

Sitting next to Williams, O'Neill and them all.

Your America was an America of the mind.
(So there was no reason to fear the flight).
Your America was where Charlie Parker was always sharp shooting
   pool,
With Humphrey Bogart in a room behind a neon bar.
Where Chet Baker never jumped or fell; he just flew, man!
He just flew away.
Like you.

So you're off then, David?
Back up the bumpy road,
Turning the corner round the Little Egyptian cottage
Navigating the reeds of Isis,
Long past the close of time.

A brown duffle coat ship, bobbing on an unpaved surface,
Weaving a few thoughts into your
Captain's cap.
(Can you tell me David:
Were you X Centric or
Merely Eggs Essential?)

How about this time I tell you :
The spark was always there, David.
But not like Daedalus, like Prometheus.
The living punishment of Truth,
Chained to your bar stool,
That eternal pint of Carlsberg gnawing at your liver.
Like Prometheus, David
The spark is always here.

For my friend David Halliwell.
I can only miss you when you're gone.

March 30th, 2006

Crawborough

DAVID HALLIWELL

An extract from *Tom in Pam and Pam in Tom*

TOM	Yes she
PAM	he was so gentle
TOM	and affectionate
PAM	I'd really like
TOM	to make amends.
PAM	I'd like to apologise to Tom
TOM	apologise to Pam.
PAM	But there's nothing
TOM	I can do about it.
PAM	No.
TOM	Nothing.
PAM	He wouldn't listen to me.
TOM	She wouldn't see me.
PAM	I remember the last time I saw him.
TOM	The last time I saw her.
PAM	I'd run in
TOM	stalked in
PAM	from the
TOM	garden
PAM	and gone upstairs to pack.
TOM	and poured myself a drink.
PAM	And when I
TOM	she came down
PAM	he was sitting at
TOM	she stopped by the table,
PAM	in the soft grey light
TOM	of the afternoon,
PAM	and he put down his glass
TOM	and she looked in her bag
PAM	with a
TOM	how can I describe it?

PAM	A precise deposition
TOM	a riffling flutter
PAM	of the hands
TOM	of the fingers.
PAM	Something so simple
TOM	and ordinary
PAM	I'd always
TOM	taken for granted.
PAM	Something I'd seen him
TOM	her do a million times.
PAM	And now I'll never see him
TOM	her doing it again.
PAM	It was the
TOM	last thing
PAM	I saw him
TOM	her do
PAM	before I
TOM	she left the house
PAM	for the last time
TOM	the last time.
PAM	I went through
TOM	to the gate.
PAM	that funny
TOM	old gate,
PAM	which has to be hiked up
TOM	before it can be opened or closed,
PAM	and I
TOM	she walked down the track
PAM	that dusty,
TOM	yellow,
PAM	rough and
TOM	stony track
PAM	called Crawborough,
TOM	just one word, Crawborough
PAM	and I looked back
TOM	and watched her going
PAM	and watched him.
TOM	she getting smaller
PAM	and smaller

TOM	going down the track,
PAM	standing by the gate.
TOM	Yes, I watched her
PAM	disappearing,
TOM	dwindling,
PAM	dwindling,
TOM	until she
PAM	I reached that point
TOM	where the track curves away,
PAM	and the house is lost from view,
TOM	just before you get
PAM	to Little Egypt Cottage,
TOM	and she
PAM	he was lost from view
TOM	and she vanished from my life
PAM	and he vanished from my life
TOM	forever.
PAM	forever.

David Halliwell died in Charlbury in March 2006. This extract is reproduced by kind permission of Liz Antcliffe and Roger Halliwell.

III

Seasons

Two September poems

BRIGID ALLEN

I

The time when a small shred of leaf
hanging from a single cobweb thread
spins, spins, then dances away
on the teeming, mote-filled air
is the time when low, dazzling light
pours gold from behind the dark tree
and the shivering cobweb is gilt
and the leaves, like our lives, flame and die.

How rich, then, the line of the woods,
how solid the shadows below,
with a grape-bloom mist in the courtyard
and long windows duskily blue.
Let the tall iron park gates stand open,
and the lake reflect bottomless sky.

II

How happy our house is
in the ruins of September!

Curled-up corpses of woodlice
shower down from the ceiling.

Violin-strings of cobwebs
draw light music from sunbeams.

Rampant tendrils of roses
trap leaves in the windows.

Hairy, purposeful spiders

pace my bedroom at midnight

while their soft-footed cousins
festoon every bookcase.

We have not slept alone here
through the white nights of summer;

they've been weaving our shroud
from suburban decay.

First day of autumn, 28. 08. 2003

JESSICA VON KAENEL

Drugged with sleep and tiredness, both,
Together like cold water tendrilling through a hot bath
Or like the strangled tangles of insomniac sheets,
I saw the first shine of the first white light
Of autumn coldness,
A square, white-shining frame...
That other light, flavoured with warmth
Of sun like palest primrose ink
May come later, may come like a reward...
That light is lovely, but this light
Is every autumn
Of my life.

Autumn is that perennial coming back to things.
Back home. Back to school, back to work,
Autumn comes bringing its rules
And its rulers. Autumn comes with its measuring sticks.
Summer hums and buzzes, thrums and pulses,
Autumn snaps. Snap
Of ice in the air, snap

Of men into suits and children into buses.
Clips
Ties on and seatbelts on, clips
Price tags off and hair off, rustles
Leaves and bags and new pages.
Snaps
Hard brilliant sky
Into place like a bigger, bluer sheet on the line.

Summer expands like a jubilant balloon
But winter contracts the horizons of the world
Almost to sickroom proportions.
Like the blessing of mild illness
Breaking like a gentle hand upraised
Into the exertions of frenzied competence...
This, too, is fussy and medicinal: a world
Of dressing-gowns and hot-water bottles.

Summer is an acquaintance, tanned from adventure
wearing little
Who turns up on your doorstep jangling bracelets
With a smile as wide as the sun... with plans
That include you, like it or not.
You like her, but do not know her very well...
And she makes you feel awkward in your own home
And you do like her, but are glad
When she is gone, suddenly, as suddenly as she came.

But autumn is a woman dressed in brown
And purple, who barges into your kitchen, rolls up her sleeves
And starts making blackberry jam on your counter
Without asking your permission.

Summer is running across the warm grass field
into the golden sun, as far as possible
out of sight.
Autumn is a homecoming.

Colours

D MOIRA WYATT

Spring was very late this year.
It shivered at the gates of winter,
Still dressed in frost and ice
and melting snow.

Until a watery sun came out,
Pulling the buds apart and
Splashing the misty ground
With yellows, blues and white
Turning our jaded eyes –
So long bereft –
To sheer delight.

Spring

DOROTHY DAY

Among the thorn hedge, birds sing
Heralds of the coming spring.
Air full of expectancy
End of winter's pregnancy.
Green spears pierce earth's brown tomb
Lamb drops from mother's womb
Soon to gambol meadows green.
'Tis a sight to be seen.

Gentle breeze blows over hill
Nodding heads of daffodil;
In garden, snowdrops, golden crocus.
Look around your eye to focus
On this sight of spring's rebirth,
This gift to us from Mother Earth.

'Façade'

D MOIRA WYATT

Fast falls the snow
and now
the pavement smooth
in innocence
imprints itself
by crunching feet.

The pile of scrap
takes on the form
of sculptured marble,
blackened trees
decaying grass
look softened, neat.

The dustbin wears
a hat of white,
invisible cars
are crouched.
Amorphous shapes
tenderly hidden,
but not forgotten,
haunt the street.

Not Adam's apple

ROB STEPNEY

This is the long-awaited week,
The one week in the year,
When the window of the gabled room
In which I strive to write a thousand words
Fills with apple blossom.

It clumps on branches
Like wet late-fallen snow
Rimmed with the pink of a dawning sun.
If every flower produced a heavy fruit,
The world would surely overturn.

The tree itself is old, perhaps has the canker.
Its forks grow moss.
Each year a few more branches fail to flower.
The autumn apples are small,
Misshapen, sometimes bitter,
Each with its own earwig,
And would never have tempted Adam.

But the tree has outlived
The purposes of procreation,
Nutrition and temptation.
It flowers now only to crown the rites
Of these seven sacred days of spring.

Autumn night falls in Cambridge

JESSICA VON KAENEL

Geese in formation:
Nature's victory-sign
From the applauding sky.

Building at night:
Birthday present of light
Banded with darkness.

Cannes: Easter Day

GILLIAN OWEN

The sky squanders rain
Soaking the streets
With a south of France
Exuberance
Alceste was not more poured upon
Perhaps not even Noah
Palm trees are shivering, if with dignity
Cats assume aplomb
There are men under umbrellas singing
Women showing more sense
But how does the light stay so clear?
Light like glass
Finding the rain implausible, impossible,
Irrelevant

Seasons

PETER HEAD

Water reeds
Talking trees
Smell of autumn
Burning leaves
Silent seas
Summer breeze
Colourful carpet
Of rotting leaves
Morning stars
Shining frost on cars
Screaming trees
Falling leaves
Summer comes
And Autumn grieves
Winter's sharp
Mornings dark
Bright silver spiders' webs
Litter the park
River weaves
Rotting leaves
Spring appears
As summer nears
From winter freeze
To summer breeze
Autumn comes
As summer leaves

Farm Portrait 1880s

PATRICIA HUTH ELLIS

I want you to imagine me as a potato-picking wife
dressed in clogs, a woollen shawl, a woollen shirt.
I stand on stony ground with my riddle and my knife,
put potatoes in my apron, worn above my skirt.
And that is my husband, wearing an old cloth cap
over pale face and wistful eyes, digging with our son,
while coughing Sarah holds the baby in her lap
who cries, in small voice, until our work is done.
Our house is cold, dark, and full of mice,
the grind is hard, the winter weather harsh,
the damp oozes from the walls, and we have lice,
the lonely peewit calls from the eerie marsh.
But, at dawn today, I heard a blackbird sing
and hope arose at the thought of coming spring.

IV

Beer and cricket

Vicar's ruin

ROB STEPNEY

Charlbury's Beer Festivals (motto: Walk In and Hop Out) have raised more than £35,000 for the community. The following short verse mentions fourteen of the sixteen excellent real ales enjoyed at one of the events. No disrespect is intended towards vicars, or grannies.

Strip and at it, Best Pride of Pendle,
Titanic White adder Friggin in the riggin.
Scorcher! Sunfire!

Pooh Pitchfork!

Bitter, Granny wouldn't like it.
Old growler, Old buzzard.
Old tosspot!

Something stronger

JOHN LANYON

(In the beginning is)
the word
the wort
the seed in the beer
the flower in the hedge

I lay the words on the floor
unprocessed, raw, rich, extravagant,
shimmering, burnished,
heavy with nuance

words like cider apples

bruised and pressured
bitter and sweet
warm, wet, waxing

I tend the fire
I watch the still

In the dark
word-drunk and sleepy
I reach you
a glass
bootleg and moon-shone

Our local

ADRIAN LANCINI

The good ship Rose, harboured in our town
A vessel within a vessel, here be found

to travel through finest ales and without destination
to travel on laughter and fine conversation

hours are killed before our very eyes
murder a pint
finish off a wine
and before you know it…

it's closing time

so good ship Rose, sail on…
and on, and on…

like Ariston,
the advert from the early 80s.

Fire and Ashes: 2005

ROB STEPNEY

Vaughan's phlegm fires Flintoff
And, when flints spark, even age-cold Ashes catch alight.

Strauss flowers
The hairy Hoggard shows his well-timed flair
And Bell peels catches from short-leg mid-air.

Giles weaves with all the wiles of Spain's ballfighters
Pietersen plays planets with the battered leather
And Jones the gloves and Jones the ball
Sing in Harmison to it all.
But it's the latter's one-fingered slower fling
That really makes stumps rear.

Then there's that risky run,
Too little thought.
'Howzat?' ask England
And the answer's 'Out'.
No racing heartbeat of a doubt:
The Aussie captain is caught short.

Ponting's tantrum tires,
But there's no bloke without ire.

Colling wood have fought even more
To keep the Aussies from the door.
But spare a thought for Anderson,
So close but far from all the fun.

Tall Trescothick stood his ground,
Though Man of Corn he be,
Unbending in the storm of wild McGrath,
And even of Brett Lee.

The like of this we will not live
In several lifetimes more.
Despite the guts and balls of Warne
From Oz the Ashes fairly shorn,
And all downunder mourn.

Not just a memory but a living

BILL PARSONS

Such is the pleasant natural scene of the valley.
By this river and on these hills man has made his home.
How green is thy valley, from its hillside I dream,
Across meadow and stream to what might have been.

The winding river I did share
With jar and line without a care.
The soul of a past time and recreation lies here,
The cricket ground to which I hold most dear,
For as a boy I did pray
That one fine day I would play.

He who would feel the spirit of the past
Stirring within him
With the beauty of the present all about him,
Has only to come as I have done,
To the cradle of my being and the foundation of my doing.
The cricket ground.

From the 1979 Street Fair programme.

V

Anger

'Naomi'

BELLA HEWES

Age six, starved of love, neglected,
Naomi eats her mother's anger and pain.
Youthful wide eyes watching
her beautiful bruised body
beaten again and again.

Shrinks from her father
when he rages;
veins swell, fists flail.
Mother tries to protect her daughter
and fails.

At sixteen, Naomi lures men and boys
who pursue her for her body.
When they're close, spits fire.
Only the burnt enter her space.

She makes weekly visits, alone
to mother, safe in psychiatric chains.

Tormented within,
Naomi splits the soft skin of her thighs
with the razor's edge,
to stay alive,
to stay sane.

Frustration

M Mayhew

The younger one
Is in a temper
Again.
Some experiment
He saw on television
Will not work out
For him.
Will he learn
A subtle lesson:
Life is like that?
I do not know
Right now
I do not care.
My blood is rising
My brain is racing.
Do something!
Help me   help him
Divert this storm.
Let's have some calm
For a little while.

Falluja-in-Charlbury, a trilogy in search of a quartet

Nick Owen

*I first heard of Falluja a little time after the illegal invasion of Iraq. I read
of a small town 70 miles north-west of Baghdad, and equated it with our
town 70 miles north-west of London. Fallujans had not resisted the
Americans entering their town. But when the troops occupied their primary
school the people gathered peacefully to protest.*

*I have watched the story of Falluja unfold from more or less peaceful
aquiescence, to violent resistance and ultimate devastation. I look forward to
the day the city is rebuilt by and for its own people, when I can turn this
trilogy into a celebratory quartet.*

Falluja-in-Charlbury

Dazzle-blue dragonflies
A dance of delight
Among yellow flag iris
Soft haze of summer by the water's edge
Arcadian Oxfordshire
Cool waters slipping silently through Cotswold stone

A moment away
In cyberspace
Cavalier copters clash and crash
An unholy mating
Death in the desert

Closer still
Not even a breath away
In a parallel universe
The copters have landed
Safely on our Playing Close

These young missionaries
Schooled in a games-of-war Arcadea
Chew gum
And slither through the streets

A base they make of our primary school
A place of safety

Big boys, fearsome toys
Uncertain of their liberator status
Settling in
They don't seem to understand
We want our school back for our children
As yet uneducated
Into politicians' death squads
Into weapons of your war

Charlbury folk
Famous in the County
A dash of colour splattered on the uniformity
Of Oxfordshire's dull Tory blue
March in protest to our school

Fifteen dead today
In this parallel universe
We wanted our school back
For our children's future.

A vast peaceful army of protesters had marched through London to protest against the illegal war of aggression. It made no difference. The war went ahead. By the autumn the occupation was a fait-accompli. Our local anti-war group had disbanded. But the Fallujans refused to submit. An American helicopter was shot down. Fifteen Americans were killed. I wrote a second poem.

Falluja-in-Charlbury revisited

The old man
Waves
Twisted stumps of steel into the sky
Abuzz with whirring mosquito men
Agitated Americans
Flash by in their copters
Trigger unhappy

A big one is down
Down
Down

This bird will no longer fly
This eagle will not command
Their skies again

The Fallujans have brought down a big helicopter
15 Americans are dead
Revenge is sweet for some
A strange poetic justice

In Charlbury
The kingfisher dives into the stream
The swallows have fled
War seems to be over
The rebels have disbanded
The banner that stood before Parliament is gone

We wave nothing
Either in anger or in greeting
At the American planes flying in from the Gulf

We place no masks of Bush or Blair
On our bonfire festival effigies
We are more successfully oppressed
Than our angry Arab brothers

Today
Guy Fawkes is an immigrant burned on the cricket ground

We will keep on burning
His impiety
Full of shallow good cheer
His fight for freedom
Burnt out
Like our indignation

It has taken months to find a way to write this poem. This was the Guernica of our own time. In quiet rural Britain it is almost incomprehensible, unimaginable. The destruction of the city of Falluja, and the removal of its 300,000 people in November 2004 is the equivalent of emptying Oxfordshire and destroying Oxford.

Falluja 3

Lead bellied blackness
Heavy rain
Clouds rushing westward
Bombing through my lovely countryside

They are born out of the eye
Of a most savage storm
How they oppress
Oppress

My life
My world
My Wychwood forest
A dreadful mess

This is no battlefield
Only fox and pheasant are slaughtered here
Yet
I am
And we are all
Among the fallen

With faltering steps, Gill and I stumble forward
Bewildered
Stammering

The forces of a vengeful biosphere
Like an evil empire's army
Have swept with awesome power through these trees
Now the storm has left us
We struggle through this smashed-down landscape
Sycamores, like unarmed soldiers,
Hacked off at the knees.

We can find our way safe homeward
This is not Falluja
This was not the will of Man

I try to comprehend
The annihilation of a city
And the suffering of its people
I witness
What I can.

2 towers falling

Igor Goldkind

This image gets replayed over and over on my TV. Smoking tower 1, itself a drama, is the first thing I see. I'm not sure what I see. Then the second plane square dances around tower 2, an arc rounds the waist and then fire, grey smoke and death. A second before I felt life, some mind on the plane I could argue with and then, a second hand reaches a second: nothing.

One tower collapses in on itself and I keep looking for the segue to Bruce Willis's smirk, something to remind me that these are just images; fantasy, not reality. And then reality, that building, completely collapses in on its own foundation. And then the second tower falls; this beautiful, angry grey flower unfolds its petals and resigning, not dying, buckles at the knees.

1 and 2.
There will be thousands.

This image is the resonant one. It is the one we will see for the rest of our lives whenever we look at Sep. 11. This is the historical record imprinted on our retinal minds, time coded and dated. Courtesy of the Networks: channel 1 and channel 2.

9.11.01

More numbers, but even the Mayor won't calculate. Abstraction gives no comfort here.

I feel the clumsy, collective grasp for meaning. The image will need to be reconciled. The shock and grief will stream towards anger. There will be retribution and I'm afraid. I'm afraid that intense, massive death is like a fever and it will boil our minds with even more incomprehensible death.

I'm afraid of American wrath.

I know I must learn lessons.
1. Everyone is vulnerable. There is no moral precept, value or nationality that will ever shield you from a bomb and its innate motive to expand.

2. The world is so small that any political event or tension anywhere, only appears removed. It can hit us all in our homes and in our offices, anytime anywhere, regardless of geography. Therefore, the world, its suffering, its poverty, its inequity is ours; not for altruism, for survival.

1 and 2.
The smoke is so strangely textured, so many shades of brown, grey, black. The ash is white. The faces of staggering witnesses, white-faced African Americans, holding hands up to fend off cameras. Once, I was a boy walking through warm drifts of white volcanic ash. I see the cameras that are here, not in Somalia, or Serbia, or Kurdistan, Cambodia or the Congo, but here, in my living room. How can it be a living room, this close to death? I keep seeing a miniature nuclear bomb, a tall mushroom of dust folding in on itself, beautiful under a pale half moon.

I feel so cold; I miss the Manhattan skyline.

In England, the TV light has frozen everyone into shocked statues. This is Medusa with a thousand hissing antenna. The English electrician keeps darting his eyes from the screen to the side of my face. He wants to know if I know anyone. Anyone that is no longer there.

When I pick up O from the nursery, I break. I can't help but clutch at her and shield her from the billowing smoke, the torrent of white ash, the blast, the numbers. All those numbers and images and fear in my mind. The world is so small now; I can count it on one finger.

O is 3.

O thinks everything on TV is pretend (because I told her so), so her mind registers images that just mean 'building fall down'; we have yet to broach the plural. She's right of course, it is pretend; otherwise, how could I keep seeing the same towers, 1 and 2 and fall; and 1 and 2 and fall; and one and two and fall and fall and fall? How can I keep seeing that plane curve gently round the tower's waist, 1 second, life, 2 seconds, gone.

Now there are the voices and faces of New York City. Tough-fed men and women trying to balance before the camera. Recount, recount, recount. 'I saw 15, no 14 people jumping from windows'. Tough man, correcting himself, grasping at numbers. 500 firefighters, 200 police, 50,000 office workers, 10 million residents. . .

The numbers aren't going to help. 4 planes, 2 towers, 2 cities . . . The numbers are going to make it much, much worse.

We are better off in shock before reason makes its plans. Reason calibrated the plans in the first place.

This is the grief before the anger, for which there is no number. God protect us from the anger.

Death and religion

PETER HEAD

Face down in a desert, a door in the sand
I open it up to see another land
Where the skies are green and the grass is blue
So many people left behind but I'm thinking of you
On the horizon a castle with a big gleaming gate
Where people waiting to be reunited patiently wait
I want to come home to you when I see you cry
I can't go any further, I'm too young to die
I wanted to come home, I can see something inside you has died
I wanted to come home to comfort you when you cried
The doors closed up and I can't get home
In all my life I've never felt so alone

In a place with no colour red
No guns, no war, no pointless bloodshed
I'm in a new place where nobody hates
No blood, no bombs, no United States
No rich, no poor, no struggling nation
No starving children trying to get an education
I wanted to come home but I'm stuck the other side
Look to the future, make the most of your lives
I wanted to come home to you, make you my bride
But I couldn't find the door and I'm trapped the other side
In a new place where hate becomes fire
No fighting, no religion, no Holy Messiah
No AIDS, no famine, no poverty to consider
No power to be won by the highest bidder
No world domination, no public to gag
No Stalin, no Hitler, no American flag
No banks, no inflation
No media coverage or television station
No government, no spin
No elections to win

No bullying, no rejection
Only love and affection

Under the eyes of gods
War makes money in wads
Powerful men playing life like it's chess
Time to look at what you're doing, the world is a mess
More to life than hate and bloodshed
When there's people to be saved and children to be fed
More to life than blood and hate dread
But into a war our country's been led

Face down in the desert, no-one to lend me a hand
We're fighting for oil in someone else's land
Think like us or a bullet in your head
Forgive those who trespass against us, give us our daily bread
In the name of Christianity, too many bullets have been shed
Think like us or a bullet in your head
In the name of Christianity hundreds of millions are dead
He's not one of us, fill him full of lead
Death and religion intertwine
We've been fighting each other since the start of time

The land is free

PETER HEAD

Land of the free
Yeh, they nicked if off the Apache
Yeh, land of the free
Land of the idiot
The revolver the symbol of freedom
Used to take the land off the Indian
Chasing the buffalo across the plain
Until they put up fences and nicked the country from which the
    natives came
Killed off their buffalo to make them hungry
This is the basis on which they built their country
The only place you'll find the Indian is on the page of a book
Killing is the path we take and it's the path our ancestors took
As many wars in the future as there were in the past
Can't we learn to get along, share a country so vast
We pretend we're a civilised culture
We see what we want and take it like a vulture
The last stand of the battle of little big horn
This was the basis from which the United States was born

VI

A rich miscellany

Haiku is a form of poetry developed in Japan. Some definitions require a precise number of syllables, and a reference to the seasons. More generally, a haiku has three lines: the first and second develop a thought, feeling or sensory impression, but the last line changes the perspective.

From my haiku box

JOHN LANYON

By the frozen lake
I touch a leafless willow
Paintbrush for the sky

       A rose cuts my skin
       In the neglected garden
       Hungry to see you

The wind in the trees
The hum of my computer
A space for your breath

       Footfalls at midnight
       Across the wooden floorboards
       Sounds from my guitar

Her thick coat of grass –
She left it off all winter
Like a strong-willed child

       The wood's grain
       The waves of the sea
       A new boat

Naked branches
Against the evening sky
Not quite black

A small split
In the back of her party dress
Only I saw it

Breakfast fruit
Freshly squeezed
Just like my girl friend

The old doors
Made by hand
Open the past

The caretaker's geraniums
Filled the wide window-ledges
Of primary school

He cut all the wires
Inside the washing-machine
I'll show those Germans, he said

Nothing on my back
Carrying the harvest moon
All the way home

Winter pond
So silent
So still

A medley of haiku

DAVID WHITTAKER

On the strike of three
   Bathroom porcelain glints
The sad face of the moon

      Thunderous storm
       Flash floods
      Frogs croak by the rusty shovel

Close of short day
   The solstice glow
Ignored by frantic shoppers

      Harbour lights twinkle
       Cloud galleons drift
      Across the silver sea

Deep lake calm
   Abandoned broken oar
A loud belch from an insouciant seal

      The sea's crescendo
       Wind hugging gulls mock
      There goes my new hat

Summer swelter
   Lakeside heat-haze
A cool flotilla of swans

      Heavy morning frost
       Branches bare
      The wren full of song

It's a mistake to look in the mirror

ROB STEPNEY

A thickening at the waist
A brow neatly furrowed
But there are championships in ploughing

Haiku

KEITH TUDOR

Quietly flows Evenlode,
Washing bullrushes
And timeless conversation.

Boat haiku

MICHELE NAYMAN

A boat without oars.
Winds toss it this way and that.
Have faith in the waves.

Books and spaces

GILLIAN OWEN
(Winner of the World Book Day Prize 2002)

On my bookshelf now
My books lean
Now there are spaces
Then, shelves were stuffed
Tight, rigid, no openings
For others
Spaces had to be found. Books
Were crammed in and
Rarely opened and rarely read
Now, there are new books
And empty spaces

I love my lamp shade

GILLIAN OWEN

She is a girl, a pearly, swirling, glowing, girly
Sits so still but so wants to be whirly.
Thinks a bit of Art Deco style
Can beguile
And hide
The tacky, tactile trollop inside.
Even still, she still knows
It is no good being incandescent
Knowing you have the soul
Of a lampshade, inside

Dangerous outside leaning

ROB STEPNEY

This was written in a sleeping compartment on the 20.30 from Munich to Florence. The train arrived at 05:17, two minutes early. It is in my native language of Esperanto.

A rectangular bed in a small square box,
In a carriage that's a clickety can

One small cell with
Five sets of prohibitions on the walls
(A bit like Leviticus)

Almost a prison on wheels
Except the guard says lock yourself from the inside

If I don't do that
Who might I meet?

Better bolt myself tight with my musings

And the door stays firmly
'Fermé, zu, chiuso, shut'

On the wall a socket
'Electric shaver only
Will not be responsible for improper use'

(Haven't you always wanted to use an electric shaver improperly?)

From the menu I order a 'spuntino freddo serale*'
(Daring since nothing tells me what the asterisk may mean)

The light evening dinner comes with an arancia drink
(because you're not allowed the water from the sink)
a drink con vitamino, calcio
e fosforo

For those who want a light

But rauchen is verboten in the compartamiento overnight

L'usage du cabinet WC
est interdit
in stations
(Lest those working underneath
Get it in the eyes and teeth,
And that would sorely try their patience)

On the window
'E' pericoloso sporgersi'
(Goodness, don't you sometimes long to sporgersi?)

'Nicht hinauslehnen!'
For any Dummkopf riding for a fall
But better pay attencion
Since sans Kopf is no arrival at all.

The worm

DOROTHY DAY

I am but a lowly, humble worm
My task each day the soil to turn.
Also, I'm very sad to say,
Part of Nature's food supply.
Nocturnal badgers' favourite meal,
I do my best to conceal
Myself from his nightly forage
Beneath woods' leafy garbage.

By day, the gardener at work
Exposes me by turn of fork.
Blackbird's eagle eye espies
Me laid there without disguise.
A frantic tug of war begins
Which nearly always ends
With him triumphant winner.
Alas, poor me, his humble dinner.

Being forty

EITHNE DILLON

Now that you're forty a chapter is done
Now that you're forty a new one's begun
So sing when you're happy
And laugh when you're sad
You'll find being forty just isn't too bad!

Homesick

EITHNE DILLON

Darkness falls and with it brings thoughts
Of gloom and deepest melancholy.
The fire flickers in the hearth
And light will visit the earth no more.
Soon this fire will fade, and with it many living fires may die
Never to be re-kindled.
Cold, still, bemusing,
Full of haunting secrecy, bereaving.
When we will leave again
We shall see happiness, share in laughter.
No more shall we witness the rigours of this world,
But round our fading fires shall sit in complete unity
Happy in our home.

On first looking into the oriental chill cabinet at Waitrose

JOHN LANYON

Susie, roll the rice,
Form a mutant teenage Liquorice Allsort,
A distant runt-cousin of a Swiss roll.
Let's have it in black and white –
You see, I'm a stranger here myself.

Susie, roll me your sushi
Sharpen the blade
Perform the rite, just for me
Show me the eye of the cucumber
A little vinegar for my rice
A dream of ginger.

Taking off the lid
I discover your miscellaneous
Drug-baron like micro packages
The green plastic fern
The plastic fish that squirts soy sauce.

I wouldn't have bought you
If you hadn't been reduced
You cut-price Samurai
A dream of skill and love
Swimming round the kitchen
A little fish out of water.

Cyprus

PETER BARBER

I

'Earthquake weather' the waiter says; 'coffee or tea'?
And indeed as we unscramble eggs the sea below
Comes to a gentle boil.
(We are sitting on faulty earth which reorganises, repercusses.)
But we are not moved, and request the former.
Sky clear, sky-blue above
The horizon due south has clouds stacked:
Could that be Egypt?

II

Safari: too grand a name for a day's shaking in a Land-Rover.
Distant headlands in binoculars,
A scramble on sands to see where turtles were,
A green valley grove full of grapefruit
Picnic amongst the scrub
Back by teatime.

III

There is another Cyprus
At the far side of the bay, under the mountains.
Lemon groves here, fruit for the taking,
Lemon groves there, fruit forbidden.

IV

She rose from from the sea
The goddess who sowed this fertile land
And men came to touch her spot.
But now at Aphrodite's Well
She gives a mere trickle

Love is fickle
Dying when the heat is on.

V

Go and see Leda
(And the swan).
But don't walk over her,
(She was anyway no walkover)
As patrician Romans had.
Just stand behind the rope
And note the sensual shake of plum buttock
Stroked by the mosaicist's hand.

VI

Herodotus
On location, more or less, a good read.
Pabulum, taken with a pinch of salt.

Voyage into the unknown

JANE CORBETT

On a journey
Across the sea by night
The stars are raining down light
across vast sweeps of time to

this moment now
and I am glad they at least are
more fixed in the inky sky
than the pulsing surface of the sea

I'm trying to find a steady path
across the buffeting of the waves
with the salt stinging
a hundred small cracks in my hands

and a glistening silver trail
left behind in my wake
my hand holds the rudder
not fast but firm

eyes scanning for where
sea meets sky
And the earth curves away
into the coming night

and for once the wind is with me
the small craft climbs up
surmounts each wave and tips down
carving a path through the teeming waves

I hear other voices
out on distant boats
laughing and murmuring
just out of sight

and fly on past shoals of silvery fish darting
up out of the water
into the glance of the moonlight
and spiralling down to the depths

a warm breeze carries me, wafts me
unresisting across the waves
dancing not drowning tonight

Dvorak at sea (On watch)

FREDDIE JONES

The sun stints a lace of fretful light,
And grey reclaims the corpse of day.
All, all around in sullen discontent,
The clamorous sea shouts note
Of fearful sovereignty.

The small machine makes hostage of my ear
And into its cathedral space
Now crowd bright monuments of sound.
And now,
The wake,
Garlanded in silvering,
And all, all is gathered up
In universal harmony.

The train mumbled on (Fear of silence)

FREDDIE JONES

The train mumbled on.
And we sit chastened
By the honeying light
Of an Autumn's late conceit,
Rapt in marshallow singularity

Where now the worried striving,
The furious flourishing of steam,
The iron rhythms of the past,
Shouting our insistence,
Drumming our defiance
Of time, of space, of now?

Gone, all gone, and, now,
Denied the corrugated shelters
Against I am? how long? and why?
We switch on the ubiquitous
Heart-beat of the bass guitar,
And shout our panic into little cells,
'I'm on the train'.

The cat

D Moira Wyatt

The cat is getting old, poor thing,
    and very thin.
His stalk is humped and stiff.
    The birds laugh
in their high-pitched way
    and mock,
And he just stares offended
    yet proud,
Saying to himself how fierce
    he once was.
No mouse came near, nor rat
    nor alien cat
Into his territory. Yes, a dog
    he chased away
Menaced till it fled in terror,
    and sad too.

The blackbirds who nest in the bush
    will not be there
To breed this year.
    When death stalks
the cat, which of the nine lives
    lives on?
The hunting cat, so lithe and taut
    or elderly cat
head down, wearily climbing trees
    to Heaven?

This poem was first published in Wychwood Writing *(1979), a collection of prose and verse from members of the Charlbury Creative Writing class.*

News flash

ROSA YOUNG (FEBRUARY 1986)

Car smashed through Post Office window, demolished a display stand and came to rest inches from the shop counter.

There is nowhere like the Cotswolds
To go out for a drive.
Thought Mrs Clarke of Radley, 'It's
So good to be alive.'

'I'll do a little shopping
And what is even better
I'll take a drive through Charlbury
Then I can post my letter.'

The screech of tearing metal,
A plate-glass smashing din.
Post Office staff leapt madly as
Their front came crashing in.

And Mrs Clarke of Radley,
Wrapped round her own headlamp,
Was heard to murmur faintly,
'I only came in for a stamp.'

Will not make you safe

Michele Nayman

A poem
will not create you.

A kiss
will not make you safe.

A parking meter
gives you time
but makes you pay.

A tree will shake
its branches for you,
never know your name.

On Poet's Day

EITHNE DILLON
Poet's Day, 6 October 1994

On Poet's Day there's none so fair
As William McGonagall from 'up there'.
His days were spent by the River Tay
Trying to work out a simple way
Of writing a poem about the disaster
(You remember the one many years in the past(er)).
He never could quite get his rhymes all t'gither;
Most of his lines went on for iver and iver
And sadly he snuffed it, an impecunious man
But the legend lives on, in the words of the sang
That all of men's deeds will be remembered after they have gone
Especially, it has to be said, in his case, the last line which always goes on and on.

After the style of William McGonagall

Plumber's mate

STUART PARKER

for Diana

While Moishe, Fernando and Nabeel the Moor
beneath the great Mezquita walls,
practised accredited beliefs and odd food rituals –
Halal to some, then Kosher and for Friday fish,
but behind shuttered door.
City state flourished and drew to this unusual place,
philosophers, jewellers, mosaic makers and plumber's mates,
and made Al Andalus the place to celebrate.

But this all predates the great crusades,
now defining all beliefs and ways
which fractures friendships, dissolves, displays,
Halal to some, then Kosher but to practice – none!
So, manufacture brand new blades
from ploughshares and replace the synagogue,
the mosque – mihrab by cathedral now supplant,
and Moishe with his sephardic ways – depart!

My mother was one such victim's bride –
of Simeon, whose family the inquisition fled
to Istanbul, their refuge by narrow Bosphorus neck
spoke Turkmen, Hebrew and behind closed door,
a little Spanish from Al Andalus, though long denied.
As Ottoman power declined, he then joined
philosophers, carpet-makers, dealers and the plumber's mate
who made London now the place to congregate.

When Boateng, Krishna and Nadine went to work,
Where three hundred spoken tongues are used,
their hopes, their aims and possibilities too
were blown apart on the Circle Line at deep,

Kings Cross and Russell Square close by the park.

– but tolerance still lives on in that place where,
philosophers, dentists, porters and the plumber's mate
live together in the world's long-lasting Caliphate.

*I wrote this in Andalucía shortly after the London bombings. I had
discovered letters from my mother's first husband, a Turkish Jew from
Istanbul, who chose Spanish – a tongue used privately in exile for 400 years
– as the language of love. Córdoba was a city where all races lived in
harmony under the Caliphate. London, under Ken Livingstone, has the
same aims and of course there were as many plumber's mates in Moorish
Spain as in London today.*

It's all in the census

ROB STEPNEY

'For we should not forget the ordering of things'

I

Lord Palmerston,
Like the Emperor Augustus, sent registrars.
They came to Hay-on-Wye in 1861.
Along the road to Brecon,
Beyond the almshouse, knocking
At each small cottage door,
They find in Royal Oak Row
A seamstress, Elizabeth,
Perhaps named for John the Baptist's Mam.

Far from barren, she'd had four sons
By Henry, coachman, who died a while ago.
But there's also Alfred, born in 1852,
When she was long a widow.
If, in the desire above all to be exact,
An abrupt line ruled on a certificate
Is all the evidence of what his father's name might be,
Do you draw a blank on history?

II

In 1891, great great uncle Henry,
The second with that mark,
Was porter in a Wiltshire workhouse.
Born more than fifty years before
In Breconshire,
He'd had his fill as clerk.

The workhouse nurse was Rachel Spittle.
Among inmates, a Francis Cackhead's on the census list.
Less fittingly,
All those classified as 'imbecile' are Smiths.

III

The winds off Hay Bluff
Also blew other Stepneys south and east.
Among them the Alfred with no acknowledged Dad.
A grocer, who now choses to be called George,
He marries Emma Gowing in Trevethin.
At the wedding, his father is recorded as deceased.

 In 1878, their first surviving son
(The previous one stillborn)
Is given as his Christian names: George Alfred Shipton.
So, might the 'George' and 'Shipton' be
The record of his true paternity?

IV

Two branches up the line,
Eva, Nick and Trystan,
Grafted onto Russian-Polish stock,
Are the latest offshoots of the family tree.
But, close to its root, remains
A small and not unwelcome knot of mystery.

The art of conversation isn't quite dead

Jane Gordon-Cumming

Oh! Er, hello! Yes, we did say, when you pass, be sure to call.
And we'll turn the telly off. No we weren't watching it at all.
Though it was the World Cup Final, they'll show highlights on the
   news.
We can always read what happens in tomorrow's sports reviews.
Even though it is the thriller's final episode tonight,
We didn't really want to see it. Do come in! It's quite all right.
What if England were just winning 'It's a Knockout'? Have a seat.
Looks like rain again. Well, fancy! (Bang goes Coronation Street!)
(They'll repeat the thriller, won't they?) Would you like a cup of tea?
(Hope 'Knots Landing' hasn't finished!) Yes, it is a new settee.
What have you been doing lately? (When's the Royal Horse Show
   on?)
Spent your holidays in Margate? (David Soul's on Parkinson.)
Yes we do remember Harold – short, fat, bald chap, friend of Roy –
And we'd love to see the photos of his Elsie's little boy.
(Oh my God, we're missing Dallas!) Your hall carpet's just like ours?
(Now we'll never know who shot him!) Oh we're glad you like the
   flowers.
We would simply love to have your recipe for rhubarb jam,
And the one for parsnip jelly. ('Ask the Family''s over – damn!)
What? You think you should be going? Left the children long
   enough?
What a shame! But if you have to... (We just might catch 'Call my
   Bluff'.)
It was wonderful to see you, and how fast time has gone!
Such a shame you can't stay longer! Goodbye, then. Right – switch it
   on!

From the 1980 Street Fair programme.

Two fables translated from Jean de La Fontaine's Fables, *1668 (Book I, ii and xviii)*

The crow and the fox

CHRISTOPHER BETTS

A Crow sat perched upon a tree.
Clutched firmly in his beak, he held
A piece of cheese; and since it smelled
Quite strong, a Fox arrived, to see
Just who the owner of this cheese might be.
He spoke as follows, more or less:
'Pray, do I have the honour to address
'The worshipful Lord Crow? Please let me say
'How excellently well you look today!
'Your plumage does look smart, upon my word!
'I'm certain that your voice is just as good,
'For you must surely be the Phoenix bird,
'The brightest star there is in all this wood.'
The Crow, who can't contain himself for pride,
To show how good his voice is, opens wide
His beak; lets go the cheese; it falls beside
The Fox beneath, who grabs it. 'Dear old Crow,'
He says, 'There's something that you ought to know:
'Flatterers make their living at the cost
'Of those who listen to their flatteries.
'The value of this lesson is,
'For you, much greater than the cheese you've lost.'
Ashamed and vexed, the Crow could only say
He'd not be caught again that way.

123

The fox and the stork

CHRISTOPHER BETTS

Sir Fox went to some trouble one fine day,
Inviting Madam Stork to stay
And have some lunch. The meal he cooked was small
(He lived in frugal style); no meat or fish:
A thin ungarnished broth, and that was all.
He served it in a wide and shallow dish;
The Stork, with her long beak, try as she might,
Got none. He lapped it up, and didn't stop,
The rascal, till he'd swallowed every drop.

After a time, the Stork, to put things right
And get revenge, decided to invite
The Fox in turn. 'I'll gladly condescend,'
He said, 'to eat with you, since you're a friend';
And on the day he trots along the road,
Most punctually, towards the Stork's abode.
Once there he tells her warmly how polite
Her invitation is; how very well
She cooks; above all what an appetite
He has (as foxes do), for he can smell
A most delightful fragrance: roasting meat,
Which promises for him a special treat.
To make things awkward, though, it's cut up small
And served inside a narrow vase, quite tall,
Well suited to the Stork's long neck:
Her beak can reach right down to peck.
It's different for the Fox; his snout
Can't get the tiniest morsel out.
And finally he has to go
Back home still hungry, head hung low,
His tail between his legs, as full of shame
As if he were held captive by a hen.

Tricksters, you are the target for my pen:
When you deceive, you can expect the same.

About some of the poets...

Peter Head, aged 23, lives part of his time in Charlbury. He has worked in a recording studio and for a record label and writes song lyrics as well as poems.

Michele Nayman moved to Charlbury in 1995. She grew up in South Africa and Australia, where her poems appeared in newspapers, literary magazines, several anthologies and were read on TV. A collection of her poems, *What You Love You Are*, appeared in 1977, when she was 21. She has since published three books of fiction, the latest being *Jetlag*, a novel.

Nick Owen is a playwright, poet and photographer working on 'Poetry Pictures' about the people and places of the Wychwood. He creates 'ritual spaces', enabling people to make significant life changes. He is 55, married with four children.

Rosa Young (née Sturdy) was born in Charlbury in 1918 and lived in Crawborough. The youngest of four daughters of Frederick Sturdy, a whitesmith, in 1946 she married one of the soldiers billeted in Charlbury in 1939 from the King's Own Scottish Borderers. She now lives near Edinburgh. Her letters to Charlbury often include verses inspired by family events.

Moira Wyatt has been writing poetry since she was a small child. Her poems were published in her school magazine, and later in a booklet produced by the Wychwood writers' group. Many of her poems are about her native Scotland, early romances, and the trials of raising a family! Being a painter influences her work.

Bella Hewes was born in Yorkshire and educated at The Manor and St Helen and St Katharine's in Abingdon. She studied English with education at York University and sociology at Bristol University. Bella has a professional background in education, counselling and journalism and researches into child and adult mental health. Currently she works in London as a school counsellor.

A retired teacher of languages, **Peter Barber** moved to Charlbury from North Derbyshire in 1997.

Jane Gordon-Cumming's poem was originally written for a Charlbury writers' group. She has published short stories in magazines, and her *Education in Action* was broadcast on Radio Oxford, and is to be included in the forthcoming anthology *The Sixpenny Debt and other Oxford Stories*. Her first novel, *A Proper Family Christmas*, came out with Transita in 2005.

John Lanyon was born and grew up in Cornwall … studied German language and literature at Royal Holloway College … moved to Charlbury in 1979 … taught modern languages for twenty years … started a new career in horticulture. Music is central to his life.

Former librarian **Dee Moss** has spent twenty happy years in Charlbury, worshipping with Michael at the Methodist church. They compiled a book of stories together, then Dee wrote a novella, followed by a collection of school assemblies. She has enjoyed being on radio and TV but now mainly scribbles verse and appreciates her family and garden.

John Bowers and his wife Sue arrived in Charlbury in February 2003; they immediately felt welcome and at home. John and Sue have been Quakers for thirty years. Their journey included appreciable years in both the Anglican and Methodist churches.

Stuart Parker is an architect who lives with Maria and three children in Charlbury. Interested in ecology, he lived for a year in the Kalahari desert in a small timber self-built house. He now works in Ghana and Ecuador and is Director of the Institute for Development in Extreme Environments based at the Eden Project in Cornwall. Poetry has come late.

Sarah Geeson-Brown lives happily with husband, children, cats, sheep and hens at Walcot. She has written on the history of fairy tales, as well as contributing freelance art reviews and travel articles. She currently works at the Ashmolean Museum.

Eithne Nutt (neé Dillon) was born in Fort William and went to school and college in Edinburgh. Due to an inspirational English teacher she began to write poetry. Unfortunately, her collection of poems was destroyed in the early 1980s. It is only in recent years that she has begun to write again. Eithne is a Scottish Gaelic name pronounced 'Aina'.

Born in Leicester in 1970, **Adrian Lancini** has lived in Charlbury for five years. He loves the place so much, that sometimes, it actually hurts. Being a great believer in the three day weekend, Adrian is currently engaged in writing a book on said matter.

Bob Cockburn is a singer/songwriter who has performed often at the Charlbury Shed. He lives in Oxford, is a bereavement counsellor, and is looking for a new venture to take his life forward.

Rob Stepney has lived happily in Walcot for nine years. He finds trying his hand at poetry a welcome change from his bread-and-butter writing about science and medicine.

Jane Corbett writes poems for performance and for the page. Her work has been performed in bookshops, a museum, pubs and even a prison.

Jessica von Kaenel-Flatt spent thirteen years in Charlbury from the age of ten, where she attended local schools before going to Cambridge. She now lives in Devon with her husband, Andrew, and hopes to write novels and more poems.

Keith Tudor is a psychotherapist, and a director of Temenos, based in Sheffield, and is a widely published author in his field. Apart from some contributions to his school magazine, this is his first published poem. He lived in Burford in his teenage years and has friends in Charlbury, the tranquillity of which inspires him to write when he visits.